⫮ **W9-BCV-804**

Collection Management and
Development Guides, No. 8

GUIDE FOR TRAINING COLLECTION DEVELOPMENT LIBRARIANS

Subcommittee on
Guide for Training Collection Development Librarians

Staffing and Organization of Collection Development/
Evaluation Committee
Collection Development and Evaluation Section
Reference and Adult Services Division

Administration of Collection Development Committee
Collection Management and Development Section
Association for Library Collections & Technical Services

Susan L. Fales, editor

AMERICAN LIBRARY ASSOCIATION
Chicago and London 1996

Composition by Dianne M. Rooney in Times and Optima on a Power
Macintosh 7100/66 using QuarkXPress 3.3

Printed on 50-pound Heritage Antique paper, a pH-neutral stock, and
bound in 10-point C1S cover stock by IPC, St. Joseph, Mich.

The paper used in this publication meets the minimum requirements
of American National Standard for Information Sciences—Permanence of Paper for Printed Library Materials, ANSI Z39.48–1992.

ISBN: 0-8389-3463-3

Printed in the United States of America.

00 99 98 97 96   5 4 3 2 1

Subcommittee on
Guide for Training Collection
Development Librarians

Susan L. Fales, chair
Merry Burlingham
Cathryn Canelas, 1992–94
Jeffrey N. Gatten
Eileen Hardy, 1993–96
Irene Woo Hurlbert, 1992–93
Janet Majilton, 1993–96
Bonnie MacEwan, 1993–95
Grant Pair, 1992–94
Marcia Rogers, 1992–95
Veronica P. Swett, 1993–96

Consultant
Bonita Bryant

CONTENTS

Preface   vii

PART I

INTRODUCTION

Purpose of the Guide   1

Audience for the Guide   2

Collection Development Assumptions   2

Adult Training Assumptions   3

Organization of the Guide   4

PART II

TRAINING MODULES

1. Ethical, Legal, and Cultural Considerations   5

2. Planning   7

3. Collection Development Policies   8

4. Selection and Review Process   10

5. Approval Profiles   13

6. Budget Process   14

7. Library Department Operations   16

8. Marketing, Outreach, and Communications with Constituencies   18

9. Selector's Knowledge Base   20

10. Navigating the Network or Electronic Resources for Collection Management and Development   22

11. Overview of Collection Assessments and Evaluations   25

12. Deselection/Weeding   27

13. Conservation/Preservation   29

14. Fund-Raising and Donor Relations   31

APPENDIXES

I. Planning Worksheet   35

II. Checklist for Collection Management and Development Training   36

III. Selector's Knowledge Base: An Assessment   37

IV. Faculty Profile   39

V. Public Library Profile   40

Glossary   45

Bibliography   49

PREFACE

The genesis for this training guide came from the ALA ALCTS Preconference held in Atlanta, Georgia, on June 28, 1991. The one-day conference was entitled "Dual-Role Collection Development Librarian: Personal and Organizational Management Issues." During this conference there was a breakout section on training and continuing education issues as well as a presentation by Merle Jacob, adult materials specialist at the Chicago Public Library, which amply demonstrated how little library literature contained on training for collection management and development.

Subsequently, Merle Jacob and RASD CODES sponsored a presentation entitled "Training for Collection Development: Collection Building by Design" at the 1992 ALA Conference, which further demonstrated the great interest in this topic by attracting a large audience and a very short bibliography. Building upon this demonstrated need, Sheila Intner and Peggy Johnson edited the 1994 Greenwood Press book entitled *Recruiting, Educating, and Training Librarians for Collection Development.*

The idea for a training guide was introduced to the CODES Staffing and Organization for Collection Development/Evaluation Committee at the 1992 ALA Midwinter Meeting and was enthusiastically embraced. Bonita Bryant, chair of the ALCTS CMDS Administration of Collection Development Committee, hearing of this venture met with the CODES committee at the 1992 ALA Conference and proposed that a joint publication between ALCTS and RASD be undertaken with the guide being published as a part of the ALCTS Guide Series. Subsequently, at the 1993 ALA Midwinter some members of the ALCTS CMDS Administration of Collection Development Committee joined with the CODES Staffing and Organization Committee to continue work on the guide.

Although many libraries have written excellent in-house training guides (see the bibliography for an example), nowhere were we able to find a published guide which libraries could adapt to their own local situations and needs. This guide then is offered to collection development coordinators, selectors or subject specialists, and library administrators to assist in the complex tasks of training for collection management and development.

PART I

Introduction

Librarians with collection development responsibilities are faced with functions ranging from selection to deselection, collection analysis to preservation, user liaison to marketing, and budget allocation to fundraising. All of these traditional collection development functions are colored, and somewhat altered, by the new and challenging world of electronic information. Unfortunately, neither our library schools nor other library experiences necessarily teach a selector how to be successful in developing and managing collections.[1] With the millions of dollars spent each year on library collections and staff salaries and benefits, the training of selectors becomes one of the most fundamental functions library administrators must undertake to ensure consistent and ever-improving service effectiveness within the increasingly changing world of librarianship.

Purpose of the Guide

The overriding purpose of this guide is to assist collection development officers, in conjunction with selectors, in developing their own training program. Training activities are centered on both traditional materials and electronic collections. A secondary purpose of this guide is to assist administrators who must evaluate selectors. Administrators must help selectors determine appropriate goals, choose the means to achieve these goals, and follow up on the selectors' success in achieving these goals.

The results of applying an in-house collection development program will be to train a selector for success in his or her collection manage-

---

1. The term *selector* is used throughout this publication, although many other titles could have been chosen, i.e., *bibliographer, subject specialist, collection manager,* or *developer.* Although *selector* seems to connote only one aspect of collection development responsibilities, the contributors to this publication view the role of the selector quite broadly, as the definition in the glossary reveals.

ment and development activities in any library, no matter what its focus on collection development.

Audience for the Guide

Administrators with responsibility for training new selectors and providing continuing education experiences for seasoned selectors are the primary audience for this guide. However, we recognize that selectors will find themselves in libraries of different sizes, with varying collection development missions and emphases, and with a myriad of organizational structures in which to perform their collecting responsibilities. These factors may necessitate that many selectors organize and provide much of their own training. The guide is organized bearing these factors in mind so that it can be used as a self-training tool for individual selectors.

Collection Development Assumptions

Collection development is a core service in all types of libraries.

The cost of a library's collections and their long-term importance to that library and to the world of scholarship in general require that extensive time and effort be spent training new selectors and providing continuing education experiences for seasoned selectors.

Many selectors will find themselves building collections in subjects for which they have little or no background. Even if a subject background exists, it is not necessarily enough preparation for collection building, which requires an understanding of the individual library and its mission.

There are micro-collection development training needs which relate to a library's specific collecting and managing policies and procedures and its specific organizational culture.

There are macro-collection development training needs which relate to subject knowledge, the publishing world, structure of the literature in a discipline, research processes in particular disciplines, shifting paradigms of electronic and print media, and communication and management skills.

The selector, to successfully perform collection development and management operations, requires a knowledge of and communication with other library operations such as cataloging, reference, serials, and acquisitions.

2

Training cannot wait for in-house tools to be developed, such as collection development policy statements and collection development manuals, because selectors must function immediately in their roles. These in-house tools are an important part of successful collection development and management and should ultimately be developed.

Adult Training Assumptions

Selectors must learn certain policies and procedures before they can move on to others. This sequence can be established in-house in response to the organizational culture and the collecting needs of a particular library.

Performance evaluation must be an integral part of any collection development program.

Flexibility must be the hallmark of any successful training program. Discussions and formal needs assessments can determine what training steps are necessary for the individual selector.

The types of knowledge or task to be learned naturally lend themselves to different teaching methods. Teaching methods include reading, lectures, guided discussions, demonstrations, hands-on experiences, formal course work, field trips, and mentoring.

Adult learners learn best when they assist in developing their own personal program; the learning provides meaningful experiences directly related to their work needs; they understand why they need to know certain information; they can see the whole picture; and they are given appropriate and immediate feedback on their training experiences.

Training, to be the most successful, must be distributive in terms of programs, people, and time. Programs or steps in training should be short, and progressive and different people should train on different aspects of the process. In-house training programs must be worked out over time. Selectors need to know certain micro-collection development operations almost immediately, but macro- and other micro-collecting knowledge can be distributed over a much greater length of time.

Selectors, in conjunction with trainers and other administrative personnel, need to establish short- and long-range plans for their collection development activities during and after training experiences.

Part of the planning process will be the establishment of measurable, accomplishable outcomes or competencies.

Organization of the Guide

The guide is organized with these assumptions in mind, recognizing the need for measurable objectives, sequential curriculum, feedback, and planning. The guide is divided into teaching modules addressing primary areas to be mastered. Within each training area there may be up to three levels identified, which provide the selector with basic, intermediate, and advanced learning experiences. The modules are sequentially arranged with the premise that there are certain tasks which need to be learned before others. Of course each trainer, in conjunction with the selector, will plan the curriculum which is needed (see the planning worksheet in appendix I). The sample activities are examples of meaningful experiences which directly relate to the work of the selector. Trainers and selectors also will draw upon their own experiences and library needs to develop meaningful activities to teach the principles and tasks important for the selector to master.

The remainder of the guide consists of material which will assist in the planning and implementation of a training program and which will assist both trainers and selectors in pursuing more information on training. The appendixes provide examples of a planning worksheet (appendix I), a training program checklist (appendix II), assessment of a selector's subject knowledge (appendix III), faculty profile (appendix IV), and a public library profile (appendix V).

The bibliography contains material on all aspects of the training modules, although citations have been grouped under nine subsections in comparison with the fourteen separate training modules found in the guide. For example, the first bibliography subsection, "Overview of Collection Development and Management," includes the citations on collection development overviews and articles on ethics and legal implications of collection development, such as copyright and intellectual property. In addition, the second subsection of the bibliography,"Training," provides the reader with citations on training methodologies, library training issues, specific collection development training programs, and finally a glance at understanding organizational culture.

Training Modules

1. Ethical, Legal, and Cultural Considerations

There is a tangible benefit in terms of morale and employee effectiveness in providing new employees with experiences that help them understand their role within the framework of the organization's structure, ethics, and values. At the same time the selector must come to understand that the profession itself may raise ethical dilemmas which must be personally and organizationally resolved. The new selector, therefore, to be successfully integrated into the organization must learn these values and his or her role early.

Suggested Competencies

The new selector will understand the centrality of collection development to other functions in the library.

The new selector will understand the organization's structure and values.

The new selector will understand his or her personal code of ethics as well as a professional code of ethics. In addition, the new selector will come to understand how these codes may conflict and need reconciliation.

The new selector will understand the legal and ethical implications of copyright and intellectual property issues in librarianship.

The new selector will identify his or her level of managerial and interpersonal skills and plan learning experiences to enhance skills.

Sample Activities

Basic Level

Review the job description with the selector, discussing the various functions of the position, i.e., reference, library use instruction, community and faculty communication or outreach, collection management and development, and the time and energy expected within each function.

Review the organizational chart, the mission statement of the library and the institution, the history of the library organizationally, and the general operating climate of the institution. The trainer might assist the new selector by raising a question which can have multiple answers—"This is an organization that values . . ."—and then assisting the selector in completing this phrase in various ways.

Identify with the trainer the ethical considerations of librarianship and collection development. The trainer should assist the selector in identifying personal, organizational, and professional ethics. The American Library Association's Statement on Professional Ethics, the Library Bill of Rights, and the Freedom to Read policy could all be reviewed. The library's own policies regarding sensitive materials and a professional code of ethics should also be discussed.

Intermediate Level

Teach the new selector the basics of intellectual property and fair use within the library setting.

Introduce the new selector to the policies and procedures for copyright within the library.

Identify with the trainer managerial and interpersonal skills needed to navigate the organization. These may range from planning projects, negotiating, conducting meetings, setting goals, and managing time.

Advanced Level

Provide opportunities for the selector to enhance his or her skills through skills workshops, formal training, and committee work.

2. Planning

Planning for success in collection development activities is both an issue of time management and intellectual preparation. Certain collection development responsibilities require a deep subject knowledge, study, analysis, and reporting, which take blocks of time. Collection development activities are also challenging because they require juggling these duties with reference, library use instruction, or cataloging. If a new selector establishes a routine early, then problems of last-minute rushes to meet deadlines can be minimized, and needed intellectual preparation can be scheduled.

Suggested Competencies

The new selector will understand the complexities of prioritizing collection development activities among other library responsibilities and pressures.

The selector will establish a pattern of weekly collection development work.

The selector will know his or her competency gaps.

The selector will develop a long-term collection development plan of action.

Sample Activities

Basic Level

Assist the selector in determining a time each week to devote to activities such as reviewing exclusion slips, dealer catalogs, approval books, gift books, and reading reviews.

Assist the selector in identifying other librarians or selectors who could assist in meeting daily or weekly responsibilities for the selector in his or her absences due to illness, conferences and workshops, and teaching responsibilities.

Intermediate Level

Conduct an assessment with the new selector which would identify knowledge deficiencies in subject, literature in a discipline, publishing, electronic access, and ethical concerns, etc.

Assist the new selector in identifying the expertise and interests of other staff members and selectors at other libraries within the community, region, or state.

Advanced Level

Work with the selector to develop a three-year plan for collection development and management activities, which could include reading, formal course work, and workshops to overcome gaps and to enhance knowledge.

Work with the selector to update the branch or library profile to facilitate planning.

3.   Collection Development Policies

Collection development policies are intended to guide the selector in the appropriateness of the materials collected for his or her library. The information needed to write or rewrite a policy should broadly teach the selector the existing strength of a collection, or portion of a collection, and point the selector to the appropriateness of the current collecting policies.

Suggested Competencies

The new selector will learn the call numbers in his or her subject areas.

The new selector will understand, at a rudimentary level, the existing strength of his or her collections.

The new selector will understand how to determine the desired strength of collections.

The new selector will understand the cooperative and coordinated collection development agreements in which the library participates.

The new selector will understand how to write a policy statement and how to interpret that policy to his or her community as needed.

The selector will grow to understand the ever-changing or organic nature of collection development policies and, therefore, the process for reviewing and updating on a regular basis.

Sample Activities

Basic Level

Prepare a list of the call numbers in assigned subject areas.

Browse the collection in reference and the stacks in the call numbers previously identified.

Read the existing policy statement(s) and review the collecting intensity levels and determine if they seem accurate and reasonable, using information gained in the preceding activities.

Intermediate Level

Meet with faculty library representatives or with public library reference desk staff to review the current collection policy. Factors to be reviewed would be

- curriculum changes or community profiles such as census data changes,
- faculty research emphases or high-use areas,
- changes in advanced degrees/chosen roles,
- number of students in undergraduate and graduate programs,
- numbers of registered borrowers,
- classed analysis identifying changes in emphases,
- circulation statistics,
- reserve patterns,
- cooperative collection development agreements,
- comparative demand for various formats (print, audio, video, electronic).

Determine institutional statistics, user information, and shifts in community demographics, which would assist in updating the policy statement.

Update the current policy to reflect the changes and emphases noted above.

Advanced Level

Establish a plan to monitor either curriculum and research changes in assigned disciplines which would affect the collecting scope, depth, and intensity or plan and conduct a survey to measure user satisfaction with all or a portion of the library's collections.

Conduct a collection-centered assessment in specific areas of assigned disciplines, which will enhance the selector's understanding of the existing collecting scope, depth, and intensity.

Establish a program of regularly rewriting the collection development policy statement(s) in assigned disciplines, utilizing the changes discovered above.

4. Selection and Review Process

A selector's primary responsibility is to identify and build a coherent body of knowledge on a given subject which meets the information needs of the library's primary clients, who were identified in the collection development policies. In order to accomplish this important task, the selector, on a day-to-day basis, selects individual titles, regardless of format, which will become a part of the collection as a whole. Establishing criteria for selection decisions makes the process less of an art and more of a science.

Suggested Competencies

The new selector will understand the criteria for adding a specific title or work into the body of his or her collections.

The new selector will understand the library-specific procedures for adding a new work to his or her collections.

The new selector will utilize a group of selection tools of breadth, scope, and currency sufficient to thoroughly inform him or her of available materials in assigned subjects.

The new selector will develop a regular procedure for reviewing newly received material regardless of format or process of receipt.

The new selector will understand the cooperative collection development agreements and understandings among his or her constituent libraries and incorporate these agreements into the selection decision process.

Sample Activities

Basic Level

Assist the selector in reviewing books already received, i.e., approval, firm order, standing orders (continuations), lease books, and gift books.

Raise the following questions with the selector as a part of the review process:

- How does this title fit into the collection development policy for this subject?
- How important is this title in relationship to other works already owned by the library on the subject?
- Is there a level of use which would justify the acquisition of this title?
- How important is this publisher in your disciplines?
- What bearing does the language of the work have on selection?
- Does the library need more than one copy?
- Are there any cooperative agreements which affect selection in assigned disciplines?

Identify the mechanics of the review process. For example:

- Work out a reviewing schedule with the new selector which will ensure that all titles are reviewed in a timely manner.
- Make certain the selector knows what areas or titles he or she is responsible for and where those items will be placed for review.
- Instruct the selector on the proper method of marking forms, tagging items, or other actions as appropriate.
- Make certain the selector knows where to place reviewed and rejected materials.
- Introduce the selector to the appropriate people to whom questions should be directed.

Intermediate Level

Identify appropriate publishers' catalogs relevant to the selector's subject areas.

Identify other sources for current awareness or current trends, such as *Billboard* or the *Get Ready* service.

Review publishers' catalogs, approval notification slips, and other sources with the selector.

Apply the same questions as used above in "Basic Level."

Advanced Level

Review gift books with the selector.

Apply the same questions as used above in "Basic Level."

Review the policy on gift materials with the trainer, in addition to the collection development policy for his or her subject areas. Decisions may include:

- Identifying titles which are duplicates of titles already in the collection and deciding whether another copy should be added.

- Identifying titles which should be considered for addition to a particular collection (e.g., reference, local history, etc.).

- Identifying titles whose physical condition will require special treatment if added to the collection or those titles whose physical condition in connection with other factors precludes their addition to the collection.

- Identifying titles which are part of a set, noting whether or not other parts of the set are present or already owned by the library.

- Identifying titles which should be rush cataloged for immediate addition to the collection.

- Identifying titles which should be routed for professional or personal awareness or for other purposes as appropriate.

- Identifying serial titles which are currently received by the library and for which copies of the particular issues at hand may be needed.

- Identifying serial titles which should be considered for addition to the collection on a subscription basis.

Review titles no longer in print to determine which titles to acquire on the out-of-print market. Work with the collection development officer and acquisitions head to review specific titles. These titles may have been identified by library patrons, assessment projects, or through book loss and now need to be replaced.

5. Approval Profiles

Approval profiles are used by materials vendors to assist libraries in collection development. Libraries and vendors establish profiles of collection needs with the goal of the vendors' automatically alerting libraries when relevant publications are available for purchase. Notification may take the form of title slips or the actual shipment of materials to libraries for addition to the collection when reviewed and approved by the selector.

Suggested Competencies

The selector will know how to interpret and understand each of the vendor profiles established with his or her library.

The selector will know how to relate the vendor profile to the collection development policy statement(s) written for his or her subject areas.

The selector will understand how to establish and alter a vendor profile.

The selector will learn how to evaluate the quality of the vendor profile in providing the materials needed for his or her collections.

Sample Activities

Basic Level

Review with the selector all components of the approval profile (e.g., subjects, reading level, geographic indicators, language) and the options for each component.

Discuss with the selector factors specific to the library, such as the relationship between the volume of materials acquired through an approval profile and the overall materials budget.

Explain procedures for reviewing approval materials, including both selecting and rejecting items.

Intermediate Level

Review with the trainer relevant approval profiles using information about the programs which the profiles are to support (e.g., collection development policies, course syllabi).

Monitor with the trainer the number of titles that are identified through an approval profile to determine if overprofiling or underprofiling is occurring relevant to the available funds.

Introduce to the selector the various vendor management reports for monitoring the approval profile.

Monitor with the trainer the quality of the titles supplied through the approval vendor to determine if appropriate publishers and authors are represented.

Advanced Level

Report to the trainer on the status of the approval profiles, after an adequate amount of time to experience the above activities. The report should include:

- Information about quantity of materials identified, selected, and rejected.
- Information about the quality of materials identified, selected, and rejected.
- Recommendation regarding adjustments to the vendor profile in his or her subject areas.

6.   Budget Process

A selector, in order to understand his or her part in the collection development process, must understand the entire collection development budget, as well as his or her portion of that budget. This understanding must of necessity be related to the library organizational structure and its governance.

Suggested Competencies

The selector will understand the basis of collection development budget allocations.

The selector will understand what information is needed to assist in establishing budget allocations.

The selector will understand the library's governance position and its implications for collection development budget allocations.

Sample Activities

Basic Level

Review with the selector the entire collection development budget allocations, providing an overview of the budgeting process; the institutional goals of both parent agency and the library; and the method of allocation.

Review the library expenditure reports with the selector. Depending upon the type of library, such reports could include subject fund codes divided by serial, standing order, approval, electronic, firm order expenditures, allocations to branches, and expenditures among adult, young adult, and children's budgets.

Analyze with the trainer appropriations or expenditures for assigned subjects in relationship to other subjects and formulate questions which will be answered in a follow-up meeting within the next week.

Intermediate Level

Gather and review with the trainer the factors which are considered for allocation.

- Community- or customer-based factors, i.e., number of faculty, undergraduate and graduate enrollment, degrees granted, faculty research emphases, circulation in a specific discipline, fiction genre or type of media, community profile, interlibrary loan requests in a specific area, demographics of the neighborhood, immigrant population, and best-seller readership.

- Publisher- or discipline-based factors, i.e., the average cost of a book, media type or serial in assigned disciplines, discipline dependency on library resources, discipline dependency on serials versus monographs.

Advanced Level

Review with the selector approval vendor reports which indicate the number of titles offered and received either by approval or notification slips. If possible title-by-title reports can be reviewed which will reveal problems in specific subject areas. The selector should consult with the collection development officer to determine appropriate

15

profile changes and firm order budget changes to correct the problems discovered.

Conduct use studies which provide new insight into the patterns of usage of the collection and its customers. These studies should be developed and subsequently shared with the collection development officer. Budgetary needs identified through these studies could include preservation, purchase of duplicate copies for heavily used titles, or a shift of emphasis in the collecting patterns.

Conduct collection evaluations such as bibliography checking or collection age analysis, which may result in needed changes in the collection and consequently the budget for that discipline. The planning and development of these evaluations should be conducted in consultation with the collection development officer, and the results should be shared with the collection development officer for purposes of identification of budgetary adjustments.

Make recommendations to the collection development officer for changes in fund allocations for the next fiscal year, based on analysis of factors in "Intermediate Level" activity, above. How would the selector balance a request for additional funds with allocations for other areas?

7. Library Department Operations

To assist in the successful integration of the new selector within the organization, the library should ensure that he or she establishes communication and working relationships with those library staff in other departments or divisions with whom the selector needs to work closely. The aim is to foster the teamwork that is critical to the selector's effectiveness.

Suggested Competencies

The new selector should gain an overview of technical and other services in his or her library that support or contribute to the collection development and management process.

The new selector will learn specifically about the philosophy, priorities, policies, and procedures under which individual staff members and their departments operate.

16

When appropriate, the new selector will be trained to perform certain technical services operations which will contribute to his or her success in collection development and management.

Sample Activities

Basic Level

Determine what library departments or divisions should be visited by the new selector.

Decide which department/division and individual staff member(s) would provide the best overview of technical services for the new selector and incorporate this as the first orientation meeting.

Decide on the rest of the sequence of these orientations, having them correspond as closely as possible to the workflow in the collection development process (e.g., acquisitions before cataloging).

Intermediate Level

Meet with the trainer and either the head of or a member of each department/division involved in this training. These might include acquisitions, serials, cataloger(s) who are primarily responsible for the subject areas of the new selector, circulation, reserve, special collections and archives/ manuscripts, business manager, and supervisors of public service desks.

Determine with the trainer and each individual the best working procedures, the important contact people, and the role of the department in the collection development process.

Meet, as needed, with specific individuals whose work is relevant to the selector's subject assignments(s) or who can delineate specific operational priorities (e.g., what constitutes a rush order, how to request a standing order, or how to handle a local bookstore purchase).

Advanced Level

Determine with the trainer for which functions the selector needs to acquire more in-depth experience in order to understand thoroughly the library functions most important to collection development activities. These might include hands-on searching experience, input of order records, preparation of catalog copy, computer input of catalog copy, ordering of new serials, check-in of serials issues.

Meet with appropriate personnel in the departments identified to get hands-on experience in the processes which will help his or her performance within the organization.

8. Marketing, Outreach, and Communications with Constituencies

There are incalculable benefits for the library when the selector understands who his or her constituencies are and what and how to communicate with them. Selectors must communicate information to constituencies, as well as listen to their concerns, ideas, and expertise.

Suggested Competencies

The new selector must develop the art of listening.

The new selector will understand the nature of his or her collections to facilitate communication and outreach with constituents such as faculty members, students, community leaders, and patrons.

The new selector must understand the process and procedures for reviewing and accepting gifts from donors.

The new selector must understand his or her community and customer profile, whether faculty, students, community leaders, or patrons.

Sample Activities

Basic Level

Review with the selector the various ways users communicate with the library about its collections.

Review with the selector patron comments or suggestions received by the library to observe variety and types of communication.

Review with the selector the most recent census data and other community demographic information.

Determine the most effective methods of outreach and communication with the library's constituencies and review them with the trainer.

Establish, and review with the trainer, a list of each faculty member for which he or she has direct responsibility.

Identify with the selector any training needed in communication skills.

Intermediate Level

Develop with the selector a program which will address his or her communication training need.

Compose, in consultation with the trainer, a questionnaire for his or her library patrons which will provide information on their material and electronic collection needs.

Develop strategies, in conjunction with the trainer, for informing community of new material (i.e., new book lists, displays, bibliographies), and presentations to community groups and faculty, etc.

Arrange, with the assistance of the trainer, an introductory meeting with the department chair and the faculty library representative. The appropriate collection development administrator should accompany the selector to this meeting. The selector should prepare a packet of material containing a minimum of the following: a discipline-specific collection development policy; a copy of the department library budget; expenditure reports by discipline or fund code; an information sheet about the selector; and any guides and bibliographies which would be appropriate.

Request, when the selector is visiting with the faculty member, that each faculty member complete a profile questionnaire or update the already existing profiles.

Advanced Level

Develop, with the assistance of trainers, bibliographies, guides, home pages, and library displays in order to describe and introduce the library's collections and services to its patrons, whether they are community members, students, or faculty.

Establish a system for staying current with the teaching and research activities of each faculty member.

Meet with library boards, faculty library councils, or other library advisory or legislative bodies, and listen to their concerns and introduce them to specific services and collections in assigned subject areas as often as needed.

9. Selector's Knowledge Base

Subject expertise is central to successfully build a library's collections, although the expertise needed may vary from library to library. Subject knowledge must be coupled with the skills of librarianship. It is important that the trainer provides learning experiences which will increase the selector's subject knowledge and librarianship base.

Suggested Competencies

The selector will understand the subject knowledge needed to accomplish tasks in collection management and development.

The selector will understand the structure and publishing patterns in his or her disciplines.

The selector will understand the various tools of librarianship which are used in selection.

The selector will understand the ethics of collection development activities as a part of librarianship.

Sample Activities

Basic Level

Conduct an assessment with the selector (see appendix III for a sample assessment). The assessment could include a review of the selector's formal education, avocational interests, and previous selection work. The assessment will vary in the depth of subject and publishing knowledge needed, but it could include a sense of the structure of the disciplines, research process, key authors as appropriate (including artists, composers, performers), key resources, key publishers or distributors, and key journals in the disciplines, genres, or nonprint formats for which the selector is responsible.

20

Write with the selector a plan to fill gaps after studying and analyzing the results of the assessment. The "Intermediate Level" and "Advanced Level" activities, below, could be developed from this plan.

Intermediate Level

Explore with the selector various ethical dilemmas that may arise when dealing with materials sellers, such as accepting free meals or reduced subscription rates from vendors; playing one vendor against another to obtain better prices or discounts; or purchasing from one vendor a title for which notification was received from another vendor.

Develop a list of key publishers by scanning approval books, notification slips, publishers' catalogs, and contacting faculty or other constituencies who can provide this information. Note particular characteristics about the publisher, i.e., cost, subject emphasis, format (electronic publishing, primarily a textbook publisher, etc.), timeliness, mainstream or fringe, availability on approval profile.

Develop a list of core journals in assigned disciplines that reflect the needs of the community. These could be developed by reviewing publications such as *Ulrich's,* searching RLIN or OCLC databases under specific subject headings or keywords and noting institutional holdings, searching subject-specific bibliographies, and contacting faculty in the disciplines.[2]

Identify synthesizing sources for his or her disciplines which provide an overview to new developments in the field. This will assist the selector in understanding the structure of the disciplines and gaining a better understanding of the knowledge-creating sources of the discipline. Sources such as the *International Handbook of Historical Studies* or *Advances in Law and Child Development* are two examples of this type of literature.[3]

---

2. *Ulrich's International Periodicals Directory* (New York: Bowker, 1932–).

3. *The International Handbook of Historical Studies*, ed. George G. Iggers and Harold T. Parker (Westport, Conn.: Greenwood, 1979); *Advances in Law and Child Development* (Greenwich, Conn.: JAI Press, 1982–).

Develop a list of reading/viewing/listening advisory sources which may aid the selector in doing collection development in all formats. (Examples include: *Fiction Catalog, Genreflecting, Penguin Guide to Compact Discs and Cassettes.*)[4]

Advanced Level

Develop a reading list, possibly having the selector work with faculty or other knowledgeable individuals in assigned disciplines, and then systematically begin reading to acquire the background needed in some assigned disciplines.

Develop, in consultation with the collection development officer, a long-range program of formal education to acquire the subject knowledge needed to fill in gaps identified through the assessment. This program could include a research class to help identify sources important to the discipline and its research process; subject courses as needed; workshops; and subject-specific organizations (rather than library related), which will provide network experiences.

10. Navigating the Network or Electronic Resources for Collection Management and Development

The library electronic environment continues to change the face of librarianship and the role of the selector. The selector's primary responsibility continues to be the selection of all relevant information in assigned disciplines. The selection, however, of electronic resources is infinitely more complex than that of print sources. The selector must apply the traditional selection decision-making process outlined in module 4 and understand hardware, search engines, cataloging, training in use, and entirely new dimensions in preservation and archiving.

These electronic resources may be indexes, full-text databases, newsgroups, listservs, or Internet databases which contain full-text information or indexes. Electronic resources have increased access to information, but they have also created an

---

4. *Fiction Catalog* (New York: H. W. Wilson, 1908–); Herald Tixier and Diana Tixier, *Genreflecting,* 4th ed. (Englewood, Colo.: Libraries Unlimited, 1995); Ivan March, ed., *Penguin Guide to Compact Discs and Cassettes,* new ed. (London and New York: Penguin, 1994).

information overload. The selector's role is increasingly important in cutting through the information maze and applying rational selection decisions and organizing principles to this overload.

Suggested Competencies

The selector will keep informed of new electronic library resources.

The selector will be able to assess the information content of electronic resources and apply standards of selection to these resources.

The selector will learn to assess the quality of the resource's search engine, especially in relationship to other search engines already available in his or her library.

The selector will understand the process and procedures established in his or her library for selecting, acquiring, and mounting electronic resources. In addition, the selector will assist administrators in modifying and mainstreaming that process as electronic resources become more common.

The selector will become adept at using the indexes, databases, and Internet resources in his or her assigned disciplines and be able to teach other librarians and patrons to use these resources.

The selector will become competent in identifying and marking existing Internet resources and in some instances will become proficient in adding to Internet resources in assigned subject areas.

The selector will understand the importance of and philosophy behind selection of print or microform materials for digitization.

Sample Activities

Basic Level

Experience hands-on training with the local OPAC, through a reference training program.

Learn the basics of searching catalogs of other libraries, which are accessed through a gateway system.

Search, with the assistance of knowledgeable library staff, CD-

ROM products in assigned disciplines, local network, regional network, and national networks such as OCLC.

Intermediate Level

Identify, with the assistance of the trainer, the libraries with the strongest collections in selected subject areas.

Identify access to these library catalogs through the gateway and become proficient in searching them.

Use these library catalogs to assist in building the current collection in his or her library by identifying gaps in his or her collections.

Identify electronic discussion groups and journals relevant to collection development and acquisitions. Assist the selector in subscribing to the appropriate discussion groups and journals.[5]

Advanced Level

Surf the Internet under the direction of the trainer, and identify sources relevant in the assigned disciplines.

Develop a home page, if needed, "bookmark" appropriate discipline-related resources, and develop online and paper guides to these resources.

Scan or key information into the Internet as a part of selecting and organizing appropriate material in assigned disciplines.

Select print or microform materials in assigned disciplines for digitization, under the direction of the trainer, and guidelines developed by the library.

---

5. Electronic discussion groups such as COLLDV-L, CNI-Copyright, and SERIALST are appropriate collection development groups. To subscribe to: COLLDV-L send a message to LISTSERV@USCVM (BITNET) with the command SUBSCRIBE COLLDV-L [your name]; CNI-Copyright send a message to LISTSERV@CNI.ORG [Internet] with the command SUBSCRIBE CNI-COPYRIGHT [your name]; and SERIALST send a message to LISTSERV@UVMVM (BITNET) or LISTSERV@UVMVM.UVM.EDU (INTERNET) with the command SUBSCRIBE SERIALST [your name].

Electronic journals important to collection development include *Acqnet* and *Newsletter on Serials Pricing Issues.* To subscribe to *Acqnet,* send a message to ACQNET-L@LISTSERV.APPSTATE.EDU with the command SUBSCRIBE ACQNET [your name]; for the *Newsletter on Serials Pricing Issues* send a message to LISTSERV@GIBBS.OIT.UNC.EDU (INTERNET) with the command SUBSCRIBE PRICES [your name].

11. Overview of Collection Assessments and Evaluations

The process of building a collection in a discipline requires the skills already outlined for selecting, writing collection development policies, navigating the network, and communicating with constituencies. Central to the title-by-title decisions or the writing of a policy statement is the knowledge of the collection needs of the library's clients. How well the library does in meeting the collecting needs of its patrons can be determined, in part, by collection assessments. In-depth knowledge of the assigned collections takes the selector away from the reference desk and its sources to the greater resources available in the open stacks or on the Internet.

What once constituted appropriate collecting in a discipline or genre may now need to be redefined. Neighborhood demographics may have changed; the downtown area may now be primarily business or composed of retirees with few children; college and university programs are added or deleted from the curriculum; coordinated collection management programs with other institutions are developed or changed; collection development budgets are changed; or new faculty bring different research emphases. Collections need to meet the needs of current and anticipated patrons, and assessments place meaning on the selection process by constantly refining the bounds by which selection decisions are made.

Suggested Competencies

The selector will understand how assessments can provide the information needed to refine his or her collecting patterns, to write appropriate collection development policies, and to develop vendor profiles which meet patron needs.

The selector will understand how to identify specific collection problems which need to be resolved.

The selector will understand the place of standards as guides and measurements in assessing collections.

The selector will understand the various methodologies which can be applied in collection assessments and learn to apply the appropriate methodology to the problem identified.

The selector will learn how to conduct an assessment, report the results, and change his or her collecting practices based on this new information.

Sample Activities

Basic Level

Determine the problem to be solved by an assessment, with the assistance of the trainer.

Review planning and scheduling considerations with the selector as he or she develops a collection assessment plan:

- Identify the most critical areas for assessment (recognize that the circumstances may change the particulars of the plan, but not the concept).

- Plan each assessment so that the bibliographic searching, inventorying, or data gathering can be accomplished throughout the year. Determine the hours of clerical assistance needed, e.g., from student assistants or library assistants.

- Schedule reading, data analysis, and report writing at times of the year when other duties are less pressing.

- Identify technical specialists needed to complete the assessment.

- Coordinate the plan with any appropriate departments, e.g., the catalog department, acquisitions department, library computing services, if information or cooperation will be needed to complete the assessment.

- Review the plan annually with the collection development officer or immediate supervisor.

Intermediate Level

Identify with the collection development officer the most appropriate measures for the specific study being conducted, based upon results of the assessment.

- Assist the new selector in understanding collection-centered evaluation techniques, which assist him or her in identifying the size, scope, or depth of the collection as well as the use of a collection. Evaluation techniques include bibliography and list checking, comparative statistics, inventories, vendor and dealer reviews, storage reviews, and weeding and deselection.

- Assist the new selector in understanding client-centered evaluation measures, which assist him or her in identifying the individuals or groups using the materials. Client-centered evaluation measures include surveys of user opinion, shelf availability studies, analysis of interlibrary loan statistics, document delivery tests, citation analysis, and circulation studies.

- Assist the new selector in identifying preestablished "standards" which may be appropriate measures for collection assessments.[6]

Refine the scope of the evaluation and the resources and time frame needed to conduct this specific assessment using the planning techniques cited above under "Basic Level."

Establish objectives for the assessment.

Advanced Level

Analyze the data gathered with the trainer. The selector will need to determine if the objectives were met through the technique(s) employed; identify and compare the results with other studies that have been conducted; review the tables, graphs, and lists to identify patterns, problems, and concerns.

Write a report which should include the objectives, the reason for the choice of methodology, tables or other basic data discovered from the assessment, an analysis of this data, conclusion (including further studies if needed), action items, and appendixes. Evaluate the results with the trainer.

Determine with the trainer who should receive this report internally and externally. Follow up with appropriate library patrons and complete the action items.

12. Deselection/Weeding

Deselection or weeding is traditional in most public libraries whose focus is generally on circulation of materials and currency of information. However, academic libraries, despite building research level collections, also encounter various reasons for weeding their collections. Whatever the focus and philosophy of the selector's library, weeding is an integral part of

---

6. Some "standards" publications are listed in the bibliography under "Collection Assessment." For a more complete bibliography see Peggy Johnson, *Guide to Technical Services Resources* (Chicago: American Library Association, 1994), 138–40.

selection and perhaps its most difficult element. Selectors may weed duplicates from any collection, or they may weed from a reference collection to the open stacks, from the stacks to special collections, storage, or sale. All of these actions must be conducted with a thorough understanding of the selector's collection development policies, deep understanding of the research, reference, and general reading needs of his or her patrons, and an eye to communication with his or her patrons.

Suggested Competencies

The selector will understand the deselection/weeding policy of his or her library.

The selector will understand how intertwined weeding and selection are and will be able to plan deselection activities into his or her normal selection and assessment activities.

The selector will understand the library's procedures for deselection and will demonstrate implementation.

Sample Activities

Basic Level

Review with the selector the reasons for deselection/weeding, i.e., space, condition of the item, circulation, duplication, relevance to the current curriculum, appropriateness to the defined collection level determined through assessments, age, and accuracy of material.

Rank, with the assistance of the trainer, the relative importance of deselection factors for his or her selection areas based on existing collecting levels.

Intermediate Level

Ask the selector to browse the stacks for his or her selection areas and identify at least one area which is most obviously in need of deselection.

Have the selector ascertain the size of the collection to be reviewed and establish minimum hours per week to be used for deselection. Have the selector estimate the completion date for collection review and weeding. (This may be difficult to do until the selector has some experience in the process.)

Give the selector any established procedures for the physical handling of material, removal from the stacks, and interaction with other staff. Should there be signs on the shelves? Should any of the material be checked out? What is an acceptable time period to have material off the shelves? (If no written procedures exist, ask the selector to outline a procedure.)

Advanced Level

Review the identified section and set aside two shelves of items recommended for withdrawal from the collection. Review the withdrawal decisions with the selector and also review the material being retained. Discuss the selector's reasons for removing items from the collection and identify items about which the trainer disagrees with the decision. This process should be repeated several times so that the selector has a clear understanding of the process and gains confidence in his or her decisions. Establish whether or not the selector will work independently or will continue to have some review of the process.

Define for the selector your criteria for assessing his or her progress in doing deselection and the quality of the work done. Give the selector any written criteria which will be used to judge his or her work. The selector needs to understand clearly how the work will be evaluated. Outline any reporting requirements already in place in the institution or define them.

13. Conservation/Preservation

As collections age, there is an increasing need in libraries for preservation plans which pay attention to this process. Although a selector will certainly not have the technical expertise of a preservation or conservation officer, he or she needs to include preservation concerns in selection, deselection, and assessment decisions. The selector needs to understand the value of his or her collections, as well as individual titles in a discipline, in making appropriate preservation decisions. As a part of understanding that value, the selector should understand the types of preservation techniques available and make appropriate decisions for binding, microfilming, photocopying, or digitizing.

Suggested Competencies

The selector will understand the role collection evaluations play in helping to ensure preservation of his or her collections for present and future library use.

The selector will understand his or her role in making preservation decisions regarding the disposition of material due to deteriorating physical conditions, its retention, replacement, or changed format.

The selector will understand his or her collections and major works in these collections and the needs of his or her patrons in using these collections.

The selector will understand the various preservation priorities for his or her library and collections and will understand how to incorporate preservation into the selection process.

Sample Activities

Basic Level

Meet with appropriate conservation/preservation people in the library for an understanding of the local library preservation program and its policies and procedures. If the library does not have a complete program in this area, the trainer will review with the selector any preservation guidelines for books, microforms, media, digital tapes, and disks.

Identify appropriate background readings for the selector through such sources as the *Guide to Review of Library Collections.*[7]

---

7. *Guide to Review of Library Collections: Preservation, Storage, and Withdrawal,* Collection Management and Development Guides, no. 5 (Chicago: American Library Association, 1991).

Intermediate Level

Review gift or out-of-print books for selection decisions, working with a preservation officer. The selector should incorporate his or her knowledge of the collection as a whole and incorporate the questions raised in module 4, "Selection and Review Process."

Identify the preservation priorities for the titles selected in this process, working with the preservation officer. Rank the materials as to their importance to the collection, according to their risk and the treatment process.

Learn the financial consequences of preservation choices, and understand the cost benefit of selection and possible alternatives to binding, such as preservation photocopying, microfilming, or digitizing, while working with the preservation officer or another appropriate person.

Advanced Level

Conduct a preservation review in a selected area of assigned collections, after appropriate planning with collection development and preservation.

Identify titles which are in need of repair and preservation. Consider the criteria as outlined in the *Guide to Review of Library Collections.*[8]

Review each volume, and identify the specific preservation option most appropriate, utilizing the criteria and working with collection development and preservation officers.

Develop an overall plan for assigned collections which will incorporate preservation review and options.

14. Fund-Raising and Donor Relations

Few, if any, libraries can completely fund the information needs of their patrons through budgeted money. Library materials continue to inflate at rates far beyond the annual consumer price index (CPI), while materials budgets stagnate or lose ground to inflation. Each library must develop and cultivate

---

8. Ibid., 7–8.

strong donor relations in order to close the gap between budgeted funds and expenditures for the library materials needed. The selector has a real opportunity to enhance budget allocations in his or her disciplines through activities related to development, fund-raising, and donor relations which utilize his or her subject expertise.

Suggested Competencies

The selector will understand institutional and library fund-raising needs.

The selector will understand the relationship between fund-raising and budget allocation.

The selector will assist the library administrator responsible for fund-raising by developing knowledge and experience in working with faculty, library boards, and trustees, in identifying fund-raising needs and strategies for meeting these needs.

The selector will identify sources which could fill the fund-raising needs for his or her disciplines.

The selector will learn how to develop a grant proposal.

The selector will learn how to successfully work with potential donors.

The selector will learn how to develop long-range objectives for fund-raising which are consistent with the management of the selector's materials budget planning.

Sample Activities

Basic Level

Meet with the appropriate collection development officer to identify how his or her collections might fit into the overall development plan for the library.

Identify specific needs in assigned subject areas which are not being met through budgeted fund allocation. These could be identified through faculty or patron requests, collection assessments, shifts in curriculum and research needs which require considerable investment in retrospective and new material, entirely new subject areas with insufficient budgeted funds, or shifts in community demographics.

Intermediate Level

Identify with the selector the appropriate methods to fill the needs in the assigned subject areas identified above. These strategies might be grant applications, utilization of Friends of the Library, current donors, or identification of specific individuals who have an interest in assigned subject areas and sufficient financial resources to become a donor.

Map with the selector the strategy to implement the program identified immediately above.

Teach the selector basic rules regarding fund-raising, such as donor relations, the most effective way to complete a grant application, and the purpose and utilization of a Friends of the Library organization.

Advanced Level

Complete the initial phases of the fund-raising activity that is most appropriate for your needs: working with the collection development officer; completing the grant application; meeting with a potential donor; assisting with a Friends of the Library program or exhibit.

Assess the results of the fund-raising activity and gain immediate feedback through the collection development officer and any institutional development officers.

Explore both long-range collection development planning and opportunities to include library needs in institutional development programs.

APPENDIX I

Planning Worksheet

Selector: _____ Trainer: _____ Date: _____

This manual is designed as a guide, recognizing that each library is unique and each trainee is unique; therefore, it is recommended that the content, sequence, measurement, and evaluation be developed directly with the selector. For many selectors the material outlined in this guide will be a springboard to other ways of accomplishing the desired goal of achieving success in his or her collection management and development activities.

In a positive climate, the trainer, and other key individuals in the organization, should work with the selector and identify strategies which will enhance the selector's success within the organization. The selector should be active in developing the areas covered in his or her training program.

- Have the selector review this guide and identify areas of competency need.
- Have the selector identify any other areas of need which may not be addressed in this guide.
- Sort the training needs into areas of importance and urgency, working with the trainer, the selector's mentor, and other appropriate library staff.
- Develop training objectives. These objectives may coincide with the "Suggested Competencies" listed in the guide, but there may be specific objectives not addressed.
- Set a timetable for meeting the objectives. The timetable could be developed using the checklist in appendix II.
- Identify for each need appropriate activities which will meet the learning requirement (i.e., reading, lectures, hands-on participation, attendance at training meetings or workshops, etc.).
- Develop performance goals and expectations which can be measured.
- Build in an evaluation mechanism.

35

APPENDIX II

Checklist for Collection Management and Development Training

An integral part of any instruction is evaluation, review, and assessment of the need for additional teaching in a specific area. It is recommended that a checklist be written for each selector to assist the instructor and the selector in assessing the outcomes of the activities conducted in each module. The elements of this checklist should include but not be limited by the following:

- Name of the module or teaching activity
- Date of the initial meeting to conduct teaching activities
- Name of the instructor or instructors
- Activities completed
- Problems discovered and recommended changes in content or teaching techniques
- Date of review
- Listing of new activities and a future review date
- Final review, if appropriate

APPENDIX III

Selector's Knowledge Base:
An Assessment

This assessment is intended for use with a new selector or with a selector who has assumed responsibility for a new selection assignment. It should be used as a tool for further training and is not intended to be a "test."

Name: _____ Date: _____

Assigned subject area for which this assessment is conducted: _____
_____

Degrees and emphasis within your undergraduate and graduate programs: _____
_____
_____
_____

List avocational interests, hobbies, or other areas of personal expertise: _____
_____
_____
_____

List prior selection responsibilities: _____
_____
_____
_____

In assigned subject areas is there a specialized subject emphasis for which this library collects more heavily? _____
Please describe this emphasis or emphases: _____
_____
_____
_____

Describe the basic research process in the subject area identified above: _____

_____

_____

Describe the ethical considerations which could potentially influence you in dealing with materials sellers: _____

_____

_____

Describe the interaction of your personal values with decisions regarding collections: _____

_____

_____

List key authors in assigned subject area: _____

_____

_____

List key publishers in assigned subject area:_____

_____

_____

List key journals in assigned subject area: _____

_____

_____

Describe the usage of serials versus monographs in the research process in assigned subject areas: _____

_____

_____

Are book review sources important in assigned discipline? _____
If yes, please list important journal titles to check for book reviews:

_____

_____

How is selection in your subject area affected by online access to database services, CD-ROM and computer reference sources, electronic publishing, fax or document delivery services, and the Internet?

_____

_____

APPENDIX IV

Faculty Profile

Name:_____ Date: _____

Campus address:_____ Extension: _____

Department: _____

Courses taught:_____
_____
_____
_____

Professional subject interests: _____
_____
_____
_____
_____

Current research projects:_____
_____
_____
_____
_____
_____

(Having the faculty member complete this profile during a personal visit will help ensure that the completed form is returned.)

APPENDIX V

Public Library Profile

The "Public Library Profile" is intended to be used by selectors to gather basic data and information about the agency and the community for which selection is being done. This form can be used as a starting point, but selectors may want to expand the types of data being collected.

Agency Profile

Branch Roles

Primary: _____ (%)

Secondary: _____ (%)

_____ (%)

For Formal Education Support Center role, list targeted ages _____

_____

_____

Total budget for fiscal year __ / __ : $ _____

Adult $ _____   Young adult $ _____   Juvenile $ _____

Total circulation for fiscal year __ / __ : _____

Adult _____ %   Young adult _____ %   Juvenile _____ %

Existing Collection

1. Print materials:
   (a) Total print holdings: _____

   Adult _____ Young adult _____ Juvenile _____

   (b) Strengths: _____

   _____

   (c) List areas to be developed and give role(s) supported: _____

   _____

   _____

   (d) List the most heavily used subject areas and give role(s)
   supported: _____

   _____

   _____

   (e) Special collections: _____

   _____

   _____

   (f) List collections relating to cooperative agreements: _____

   _____

   _____

   (g) Language collections:

   1. _____ 2. _____ 3. _____ 4. _____

   (h) Number of periodical subscriptions: _____

   (i) Number of continuations: _____

2. Nonprint materials:

   Total holdings: _____

   Audio books (adult) _____

   Audio books (children) _____

   Book/cassette pairs _____

   Compact disc (music) _____

   Compact disc (spoken word) _____

   Records _____

   Toys _____

   Videos _____

   Other _____

41

3. Special resources (CD-ROM reference services, computer-based reference sources, etc.): _____

_____

_____

Community Profile

1. List the library's geographic boundaries: _____

_____

2. Total population served: _____

3. Median income: _____

4. Median house value: _____

5. Age levels: 0–4 _____   5–19 _____   20–34 _____

   35–54 _____   55–64 _____   65 and over _____

6. Median age: _____

7. Predominant ethnic groups (% of total population):

   (a) _____   (b) _____   (c) _____

   (d) _____   (e) _____   (f) _____

8. Highest level of schooling for adults (over 18):

   Elementary school _____ (%)   High school _____ (%)

   College _____ (%)

9. Number of schools:

   Day-care centers _____   Elementary _____

   Secondary _____   Trade/technical _____

   Colleges/universities _____

10. Other neighborhood characteristics (i.e., business diversity, primary occupations, community groups/organizations, parks and recreational information, transportation patterns, etc.): _____

_____

_____

_____

_____

Customer Profile

Readership

1. Predominant ethnic groups (% of customers):

   (a)_____ (b)_____ (c)_____ (d) _____

   (e)_____

2. Foreign language needs:

   (a)_____ (b)_____ (c)_____ (d) _____

   (e)_____

3. Age groups of customers (indicate %):

   (a) Senior adult_____ (b) Adult _____

   (c) Young adult _____ (d) Juvenile_____

Reader Interests

(scale of interest: 1 = high; 2 = medium; 3 = low)

1. *Adult fiction:*

   Family saga ___ Historical fiction ___ Horror___ Sci-fi___
   Mystery ___ Psychothriller___ Spy/espionage___ Crime___
   Romance___ Adventure___ Technothriller___ Other___

2. *Adult nonfiction:*

   His./Bio.___ Current affairs ___ Health___ Bus./Fin.___
   Sports ___ Self-help___ Social issues___ True crime___
   Science/Math___ Careers___ Computers___ Parenting___
   Home design/Repairs___ Other ___

3. *Young adult*—assignment needs and interests:

   (a)_____ (b)_____ (c)_____ (d) _____

4. *Juvenile*—after school (school assignments, latchkey, etc.): _____

   _____

   _____

   _____

General comments about overall branch reader needs and interests:

_____

_____

_____

GLOSSARY

approval notification slips Bibliographic information provided to libraries by publishers and wholesalers which contains information about recent publications that fit a library's collection profile specified in terms of subject, collecting levels, formats, prices, languages, etc.

approval plan* An arrangement by which a publisher or wholesaler assumes the responsibility for selecting and supplying, subject to return privileges, all publications, as issued, fitting a library's collection profile specified in terms of subjects, levels, formats, prices, languages, etc. Some approval plans provide for the library to receive advance notification slips rather than the publications themselves. *See also* approval notification slips

approval profile Information about a library's collecting needs in terms of subject, levels, formats, prices, languages, etc., used by publishers and wholesalers to supply new publications or information about new publications to libraries. *See also* approval plan

assessment *see* collection evaluation

collecting levels A set of abstract collection qualities or characteristics used as a scale to describe or categorize collection strengths (and by extension, current and desired collecting intensities).

collection assessment *see* collection evaluation

collection development* A term which encompasses a number of activities related to the development of the library collection, including the determination and coordination of selection policy, assessment of needs of users and potential users, collection use studies, collection evaluation, identification of collection needs, selection of materials, planning for resource sharing, collection maintenance, and weeding.

---

* Definition from *ALA Glossary of Library and Information Science* (Chicago: American Library Association, 1983).

collection development policy A statement that indicates the mission, goals, and objectives of a library's collection development programs and describes the past, current, and desired collecting levels for various collections.

collection evaluation The process of assessing the quality of a library collection, usually in terms of specific objectives or needs of the target group of that particular collection; one aspect of collection development. Synonymous with *collection assessment.*

collection management* A term used to refer specifically to the application of quantitative techniques (statistical analyses, cost-benefit studies, etc.) in collection development.

conservation* The use of chemical and physical procedures in treatment or storage to ensure the preservation of books, manuscripts, records, and other documents. *See also* preservation

deselection The official removal of titles from a library's collection, as a result of weeding or the withdrawal of missing or physically damaged materials.

electronic discussion group A number of individuals who communicate with each other by sending electronic-text messages to a computer which then redistributes the messages as electronic mail to each member of the pool.

electronic resources Library materials that are available in electronic formats, which may include text, datasets, graphics, multimedia, and Internet. Electronic resources may be located at computers on-site or at remote locations.

exclusion slips *see* approval notification slips

firm order An order placed with a dealer specifying a time limit for delivery and a price which must not be exceeded without the customer's prior approval.

gateway system A generic term for computer-based methods (e.g., menus) of accessing, easily, computer databases which may be located on-site or at remote locations.

mission statement A library's statement of purpose and intent.

notification slips *see* approval notification slips

preservation* The activities associated with maintaining library and archival materials for use, either in their original physical form or in some usable way. *See also* conservation

preservation microfilming* The microfilming for preservation purposes of books, serials, manuscripts, and other documents, using for this purpose materials and processing methods of maximum permanence, and creating a store of camera microfilm which is housed under controlled conditions and used only to make distribution copies. *See also* preservation photocopying

preservation photocopying   The photocopying for preservation purposes of books, serials, manuscripts, and other documents, using materials and processing methods of maximum permanence. *See also* preservation microfilming

profile *see* approval profile

selector   Library staff member who is responsible for developing, managing, and teaching about collections in assigned subjects. Responsibilities will vary from library to library but could include writing and revising collection development policies; promoting, marketing, and interpreting collections and resources; evaluating collections and services; and soliciting funding to supplement allocated collection development funds.

training*   The process of developing knowledge, skills, and attitudes needed by employees to perform their duties effectively and to meet the expectations and goals of the organization. This diverse process, which may be performed by supervisors, fellow employees, and personnel officers, involves planning, preparation, execution, and evaluation.

weeding   The official removal of titles from a library's collection based on the value of the materials to the overall collection. *See also* deselection

BIBLIOGRAPHY

Overview of Collection Development and Management

Allison, Anne Marie. "Managing Collections in an Automated Network Environment." *Collection Building* 9, no.2 (1989): 24–32.

Association of Research Libraries, Office of Management Studies. *University Copyright Policies in ARL Libraries.* SPEC Kit 138. Washington, D.C.: ARL, 1987.

Atkinson, Ross. "Conditions of Collection Development." In *Collection Management: A New Treatise,* 29–44. Ed. Charles B. Osburn and Ross Atkinson. Greenwich: JAI Press, 1991.

_____. "Old Forms, New Forms: The Challenge of Collection Development." *College & Research Libraries* 50 (September 1989): 507–520.

Bruwelheide, Janis H. *The Copyright Primer for Librarians and Educators.* 2nd ed. Chicago: American Library Association; Washington, D.C.: National Education Association, 1995.

Bryant, Bonita. "The Organizational Structure of Collection Development." *Library Resources & Technical Services* 31 (April/June 1987): 111–122.

Bucknall, Carolyn. "Organization of Collection Development and Management in Academic Libraries." *Collection Building* 9, no.3 (1989): 11–17.

Copyright Basics. Circular 1. Washington, D.C.: Copyright Office, Library of Congress, 1994.

Cyzyk, Mark. "Canon Formation, Library Collections and the Dilemma of Collection Development." *College & Research Libraries* 54 (January 1993): 58–65.

Demas, Sam. "Collection Development for the Electronic Library: A Conceptual and Organizational Model." *Library Hi Tech* 12, no.3 (1994): 71–80.

Evans, G. Edward. *Developing Library and Information Center Collections.* 2nd ed. Littleton, Colo.: Libraries Unlimited, 1987.

Faigel, Martin. "The Library as a Marketplace in a Collection Management Environment." *Library Acquisitions: Practice & Theory* 12, no.2 (1988): 191–195.

Harloe, Bart. "Achieving Client-Centered Collection Development in Small and Medium-Sized Academic Libraries." *College & Research Libraries* 50 (May 1989): 344–353.

McClure, Charles R., et. al. *Planning and Role Setting for Public Libraries: A Manual of Options and Procedures.* Chicago: American Library Association, 1987.

Magrill, Rose Mary, and John Corbin. *Acquisitions Management and Collection Development in Libraries.* 2nd ed. Chicago: American Library Association, 1989.

Manoff, Marlene. "Academic Libraries and the Culture Wars: The Politics of Collection Development." *Collection Management* 16, no.4 (1992): 1–17.

Metz, Paul, and Bela Foltin Jr. "A Social History of Madness—or, Who's Buying This Round? Anticipating and Avoiding Gaps in Collection Development." *College & Research Libraries* 51 (January 1990): 33–39.

Osburn, Charles B. "Collection Development and Management." In *Academic Libraries: Research Perspectives,* 1–37. Ed. Mary Jo Lynch and Arthur Young. Chicago: American Library Association, 1990.

_____, and Ross Atkinson. *Collection Management: A New Treatise.* Greenwich, Conn.: JAI Press, 1991.

Pankake, Marcia. "From Book Selection to Collection Management: Continuity and Advance in an Unending Work." *Advances in Librarianship* 13 (1984): 185–210.

Reed-Scott, Jutta. "Information Technologies and Collection Development." *Collection Building* 9, no.3 (1989): 47–51.

Reference Collection Management: A Manual. Chicago: Reference and Adult Services Division, American Library Association, 1992.

Robinson, Barbara M. "Managing Change and Sending Signals in the Marketplace." *Library Acquisitions: Practice & Theory* 13, no.3 (1989): 217–225.

Schad, Jasper G. "Managing Collection Development in University Libraries That Utilize Librarians with Dual Responsibility Assignments." *Library Acquisitions: Practice & Theory* 14, no.2 (1990): 165–171.

Strauch, Katina, and Bruce Strauch, eds. *Legal and Ethical Issues in Acquisitions.* New York: Haworth Press, 1990. Also published in *Acquisitions Librarian*, no. 3 (1990).

Stueart, Robert D., and George B. Miller, eds. *Collection Development in Libraries: A Treatise.* Greenwich, Conn.: JAI Press, 1980.

Williams, Lynn B. "Subject Knowledge for Subject Specialists: What the Novice Bibliographer Needs to Know." *Collection Management* 14, no.3/4 (1991): 31–47.

Wortman, William A. *Collection Management: Background and Principles.* Chicago: American Library Association, 1989.

Training

Argyris, Chris. "Teaching Smart People How to Learn." *Harvard Business Review* 69 (May/June 1991): 99–109.

Bullard, Scott R., ed. "Educating Rita—Part II: Training for Collection Development." *Library Acquisitions: Practice & Theory* 8, no.4 (1984): 243–245.

Casserly, Mary F., and Judith L. Hegg. "A Study of Collection Development Personnel Training and Evaluation in Academic Libraries." *Library Acquisitions: Practice & Theory* 17, no.3 (1993): 249–262.

Creth, Sheila D. *Effective On-the-Job Training: Developing Library Human Resources.* Chicago: American Library Association, 1992.

Gleason, Maureen L. "Training Collection Development Librarians." *Collection Management* 4, no.4 (1982): 1–8.

Guide for Writing a Bibliographer's Manual. Collection Management and Development Committee, Resources and Technical Services Division, Carolyn Bucknall, ed. Collection Management and Development Guides, no. 1. Chicago: American Library Association, 1987.

McDaniel, Julie Ann. "Leading the Way: In-House Collection Development Training for New Selectors." *Library Acquisitions: Practice & Theory* 13, no.3 (1989): 293–295.

Nofsinger, Mary M., and Angela S. W. Lee. "Beyond Orientation: The Roles of Senior Librarians in Training Entry-Level Reference

Colleagues." *College & Research Libraries* 55 (March 1994): 161–170.

Recruiting, Educating, and Training Librarians for Collection Development. Ed. Peggy Johnson and Sheila S. Intner. New Directions in Information Management, no. 33. Westport, Conn.: Greenwood Press, 1994.

Schein, Edgar H. *Organizational Culture and Leadership.* 2nd ed. San Francisco: Jossey-Bass, 1992.

Soete, George J. "Training for Success: Integrating the New Bibliographer into the Library." In *Recruiting, Educating, and Training Librarians for Collection Development,* 159–169. Ed. Peggy Johnson and Sheila S. Intner. New Directions in Information Management, no. 33 (Westport, Conn.: Greenwood Press, 1994).

Staff Development: A Practical Guide. 2nd ed. Prepared by the Staff Development Committee, Personnel Administration Section, Library Administration and Management Association. Chicago: American Library Association, 1992.

University of Texas at Austin. The General Libraries. *Bibliographer's Manual: A Guide to the General Libraries Collection Development Program.* Contributions to Librarianship, no. 7. Austin: General Libraries, 1982.

Collection Development Policy Statements

Bostic, Mary J. "A Written Collection Development Policy: To Have and Have Not." *Collection Management* 10, no.3/4 (1988): 89–103.

Branin, Joseph. "Information Policies for Collection Development Librarians." *Collection Building* 9, no.3–4 (1989): 19–23.

Carpenter, Eric J. "Collection Development Policies Based on Approval Plans." *Library Acquisitions: Practice & Theory* 13, no.1 (1989): 39–43.

Guide for Written Collection Policy Statements. 2nd ed. Subcommittee to Revise the Guide for Written Collection Policy Statements, Administration of Collection Development Committee, Collection Management and Development Section, Association for Library Collections & Technical Services, Joanne S. Anderson, ed. Chicago: American Library Association, 1996.

Jacob, Merle. "Get It in Writing: A Collection Development Plan for the Skokie Public Library." *Library Journal* 115 (September 1, 1990): 166–169.

Osburn, Charles B. "Some Practical Observations on the Writing, Implementation, and Revision of Collection Development Policy." *Library Resources & Technical Services* 23 (Winter 1979): 7–15.

Taborsky, Theresa, and Patricia Lenkokski, comps. *Collection Development Policies for College Libraries.* CLIP Note, no. 11. Chicago: American Library Association, Association of College & Research Libraries, 1989.

Taylor, Mary M., ed. *School Library and Media Center Acquisitions Policies and Procedures.* Phoenix: Oryx Press, 1981.

Selection and Review Process

Atkinson, Ross. "Text Mutability and Collection Administration." *Library Acquisitions: Practice & Theory* 14, no.4 (1990): 355–358.

Blake, Virgil L. P. "The Role of Review and Reviewing Media in the Selection Process: An Examination of the Research Record." *Collection Management* 11, no.1/2 (1989): 1–40.

Boissonnas, Christian M. "The Cost Is More than an Elegant Dinner: Your Ethics Are at Steak." *Library Acquisitions: Practice & Theory* 11, no.2 (1987): 145–152.

Branin, Joseph J. "Cooperative Collection Development." In *Collection Management: A New Treatise,* Part A: 81–110. Ed. Charles B. Osburn and Ross Atkinson. Greenwich, Conn.: JAI Press, 1991.

Bullard, Scott R. "Tribes and Tribulations: Ethical Snares in the Organization of the Collection Management Units." In *Acquisitions '90,* 17–23. Ed. David C. Genaway. Canfield, Ohio: Genaway & Associates, 1990.

Couch, Nena, and Nancy Allen, eds. *The Humanities and the Library.* 2nd ed. Chicago: American Library Association, 1993.

Demas, Sam. "Mainstreaming Electronic Formats." *Library Acquisitions: Practice & Theory* 13, no.3 (1989): 227–232.

Dougherty, Richard M. "A Conceptual Framework for Organizing Resource Sharing and Shared Collection Development Programs." *Journal of Academic Librarianship* 14 (November 1988): 287–291.

Dowd, Sheila T. "Library Cooperation: Methods, Models to Aid Information Access." *Journal of Library Administration* 12, no.3 (1990): 63–81.

Downes, Robin. "Resource Sharing and New Information Technology: An Idea Whose Time Has Come." *Journal of Library Administration* 10, no.1 (1989): 115–125.

Ferguson, Anthony W. "Assessing the Collection Development Need for CD-ROM Products." *Library Acquisitions: Practice & Theory* 12, no.3/4 (1988): 325–332.

Guide to Cooperative Collection Development. Subcommittee on Guide to Cooperative Collection Development, Administration of Collection Development Committee, Collection Management and Development Section, Association for Library Collections & Technical Services, Bart Harloe, ed. Collection Management and Development Guides, no. 6. Chicago: American Library Association, 1994.

Hamaker, Charles A. "Management Data for Selection Decisions in Building Library Collections." *Journal of Library Administration* 17, no.2 (1992): 71–97.

Hannaford, William E. "Ethics and Collection Development." In *Collection Development in College Libraries,* 55–60. Ed. Joanne Schneider Hill, William E. Hannaford Jr., and Ronald H. Epp. Chicago: American Library Association, 1991.

——. "Tilting at Windmills: Selection in College Libraries." *Collection Management* 12, no.1/2 (1990): 31–35.

Hattendorf, Lynn C. "The Art of Reference Collection Development." *RQ* 29 (Winter 1989): 219–229.

Heitshu, Sara C., and J. Travis Leach. "Developing Serial Collections in the 1990s." *Collection Building* 9, no.3–4 (1989): 53–59.

Hewitt, Joe A., and John Shipman. "Cooperative Collection Development among Research Libraries in the Age of Networking." *Advances in Library Automation and Networking* 1 (1987): 189–232.

Itner, Sheila S. "Differences between Access vs. Ownership." *Technicalities* 9 (September 1989): 5–8.

_____. "Selecting Software." *Library Acquisitions: Practice & Theory* 13, no.3 (1989): 233–240.

Johnson, Peggy. "A Rose Is a Rose." *Technicalities* 9 (July 1989): 7–8.

Kovacs, Beatrice. *The Decision-making Process for Library Collections: Case Studies in Four Types of Libraries.* New York: Greenwood Press, 1990.

Loup, Jean I. "Analysis of Selection Activities to Supplement Approval Plans." *Library Resources & Technical Services* 35, (April 1991): 202–216.

Mosher, Paul. "Cooperative Collection Development: Collaborative Interdependence." *Collection Building* 9, no.3 (1989): 29–32.

Parker, Jean McGruer. "Scholarly Book Reviews in Literature Journals as Collection Development Sources for Librarians." *Collection Management* 11, no.1/2 (1989): 41–57.

Pitman, Randy. *Video Librarian's Guide to Collection Development and Management.* Boston: G. K. Hall, 1992.

Rutledge, John, and Luke Swindler. "The Selection Decision: Defining Criteria and Establishing Priorities." *College & Research Libraries* 48 (March 1987): 123–131.

Ryland, John. "Collection Development and Selection: Who Should Do It?" *Library Acquisitions: Practice & Theory* 6, no.1 (1982): 13–18.

Sartori, Eva Martin. "Regional Collection Development of Serials." *Collection Management* 11, no.1/2 (1989): 69–76.

Schwartz, Charles A. "Book Selection, Collection Development and Bounded Rationality." *College & Research Libraries* 50 (May 1989): 328–343.

Selection of Library Materials for Area Studies: Part 1, Asia, Iberia and Latin America, Eastern Europe and the Soviet Union, and the South Pacific. Ed. Cecily Johns. Chicago: American Library Association, 1990.

Selection of Library Materials in the Humanities, Social Sciences, and Sciences. Ed. Patricia A. McClung. Chicago: American Library Association, 1985.

Selection of Library Materials in Applied and Interdisciplinary Fields. Ed. Beth J. Shapiro and John Whaley. Chicago: American Library Association, 1987.

Soete, George J. "Applying a Strategic Planning Process to Resource Sharing: The Changing Face of Collaborative Collection Development among the University of California Libraries." *Advances in Library Resource Sharing* 2 (1991): 51–59.

Spiller, David. *Book Selection: An Introduction to Principles and Practices.* 5th ed. London: Clive Bingly, 1991.

Spreitzer, Francis, ed. *Microforms in Libraries: A Manual for Evaluation and Management.* Chicago: American Library Association, 1985.

Marketing and Liaison with Faculty, Community

Baker, Sharon L. "Public Libraries." *In Collection Management: A New Treatise,* 395–416. Ed. Charles B. Osburn and Ross Atkinson. Greenwich, Conn.: JAI Press, 1991.

_____. "The Display Phenomenon: An Exploration into Factors Causing the Increased Circulation of Displayed Books." *Library Quarterly* 56 (July 1986): 237–257.

Dittenmore, Margaret R. "Changing Patterns of Faculty Participation in Collection Development." *Collection Management* 16, no.4 (1992): 79–89.

Drummond, Rebecca C., Anna Page Mosby, and Mary H. Munroe. "A Joint Venture in Collection Building." *Collection Management* 14, no.1/2 (1991): 59–72.

Goldhor, Herbert. "The Effect of Prime Display Location on Public Library Circulation of Selected Adult Titles." *Library Quarterly* 42 (October 1972): 371–389.

Liaison Services in ARL Libraries. SPEC Kit 189. Washington, D.C.: ARL, Office of Management Services, Systems and Procedures Exchange Center, 1992.

Pasterczyk, Catherine E. "Checklist for the New Selector." *College & Research Libraries News* 49 (July/August 1988): 434–35.

"RASD Guidelines for Liaison Work." *RQ* 32 (Winter 1992): 198–204.

Wu, Connie, et al. "Effective Liaison Relationships in an Academic Library." *College & Research Libraries News* 55 (May 1994): 254, 303.

Budget Process

Blake, Vergil L. P., and Renee Tjoumas. "Determining Budgets for School Library Media Centers." *Collection Building* 9, no.2 (1989): 12–18.

Budd, John M., and Kay Adams. "Allocation Formulas in Practice." *Library Acquisitions: Practice & Theory* 13, no.4 (1989): 381–390.

Cubberly, Carol W. "Allocating the Materials Funds Using Total Cost of Materials." *Journal of Academic Librarianship* 19 (March 1993): 16–21.

Guide to Budget Allocation for Information Resources. Subcommittee on Budget Allocation, Collection Management and Development Committee, Resources Section, Association for Library Collections & Technical Services, Edward Shreeves, ed. Collection Management and Development Guides, no. 4. Chicago: American Library Association, 1991.

Lowry, Charles Bryan. "Reconciling Pragmatism, Equity and Need in the Formula Allocation of Book and Serial Funds." *College & Research Libraries* 53 (March 1992): 121–138.

Lynden, Frederick Charles. "The Impact of the Rising Costs of Books and Journals on the Overall Library Budget." *Journal of Library Administration* 10, no.1 (1989): 81–98.

Niles, Judith. "The Politics of Budget Allocation." *Library Acquisitions: Practice & Theory* 13, no.1 (1989): 51–55.

Packer, Donna. "Acquisitions Allocations: Equity, Politics and Formulas." *Journal of Academic Librarianship* 14 (November 1988): 276–286.

Ring, Richard. "Budgeting for Collection Development." *Collection Building* 9, no.2 (1989): 25–28.

Werking, Richard Hume. "Allocating the Library's Book Budget: Historical Perspectives and Current Reflections." *Journal of Academic Librarianship* 14 (July 1988): 140–144.

Collection Assessment

Aguilar, William. "The Application of Relative Use and Interlibrary Demand in Collection Development." *Collection Management* 8 (Spring 1986): 15–23.

Association of College & Research Libraries. "Standards for University Libraries." *College & Research Libraries News* 50 (September 1989): 679–691.

Association of College & Research Libraries and Association for Educational Communications and Technology. "Standards for Community, Junior and Technical College Learning Resources Programs." *College & Research Libraries News* 51 (September 1990): 757–767.

Baker, Robert K. "Using a Turnkey Automated System to Support Collection Assessment." *College & Research Libraries* 51 (July 1990): 360–366.

Bartolo, Laura M. "Automated ILL Analysis and Collection Development: A Hi-Tech Marriage of Convenience." *Library Acquisitions: Practice & Theory* 13, no.4 (1989): 361–369.

Britten, William A. "A Use Statistic for Collection Management: The 80/20 Rule Revisited." *Library Acquisitions: Practice & Theory* 14, no.2 (1990): 183–189.

Clapp, Verner W., and Robert T. Jordan. "Quantitative Criteria for Adequacy of Academic Library Collections." *College & Research Libraries* 50 (March 1989): 154–163.

Elzy, Cheryl Asper, and F. W. Lancaster. "Looking at a Collection in Different Ways: A Comparison of Methods of Bibliographic Checking." *Collection Management* 12, no.3/4 (1990): 1–10.

Ferguson, Anthony W. "Collection Assessment and Acquisitions Budgets." *Journal of Library Administration* 17, no.2 (1992): 59–70.

_____, Joan Grant, and Joel Rutstein. "The RLG Conspectus: Its Uses and Benefits." *College & Research Libraries* 49 (May 1988): 197–206.

Forcier, Peggy. "Building Collections Together: The Pacific Northwest Conspectus." *Library Journal* 113 (April 15, 1988): 43–45.

Guide to the Evaluation of Library Collections. Subcommittee on Guidelines for Collection Development, Collection Management and Development Committee, Resources Section, Resources & Technical Services Division, Barbara Lockett, ed. Collection Management and Development Guides, no. 2. Chicago: American Library Association, 1989.

Hall, Blaine H. *Collection Assessment Manual for College and University Libraries*. Phoenix: Oryx Press, 1985.

Hyman, Ferne. "Collection Evaluation in the Research Environment." *Collection Building* 9, no.3–4 (1989): 33–37.

Krueger, Karen L. "Guidelines for Collection Management." In *Collection Management in Public Libraries,* 13–26. Ed. Judith Serebnick. Chicago: American Library Association, 1986.

Lancaster, F. W. "Evaluating Collections by Their Use." *Collection Management* 4, no.1/2 (1982): 15–43.

Lundin, Anne H. "List-checking in Collection Development: An Imprecise Art." *Collection Management* 11, no.3/4 (1989): 103–112.

McClure, Charles R., et al. *Planning and Role Setting for Public Libraries: A Manual of Options and Procedures.* Chicago: American Library Association, 1987.

Mosher, Paul H. "Quality and Library Collections: New Directions in Research and Practice in Collection Evaluation." *Advances in Librarianship* 13 (1984): 211–238.

Oberg, Larry R. "Evaluating the Conspectus Approach for Smaller Library Collections." *College & Research Libraries* 49 (May 1988): 187–196.

Paskoff, Beth M., and Anna H. Perrault. "A Tool for Comparative Collection Analysis: Conducting a Shelflist Sample to Construct a Collection Profile." *Library Resources & Technical Services* 34 (April 1990): 199–215.

Sandler, Mark. "Quantitative Approaches to Qualitative Collection Assessment." *Collection Building* 8, no.4 (1988): 12–17.

Segal, Joseph P. *Evaluating and Weeding Collections in Small and Medium-Sized Libraries: The CREW Method.* Chicago: American Library Association, 1980.

Stielow, Frederick J., and Helen R. Tibbo. "Collection Analysis in Modern Librarianship: A Stratified Multidimensional Model." *Collection Management* 11, no.3/4 (1989): 73–91.

Van House, Nancy A., Beth Weil, and Charles R. McClure. *Measuring Academic Library Performance: A Practical Approach.* Chicago: American Library Association, 1990.

Van House, Nancy A., et al. *Output Measures for Public Libraries: A Manual of Standardized Procedures.* 2nd ed. Chicago: American Library Association, 1987.

Wiemers Jr., Eugene, et al. "Collection Evaluation: A Practical Guide to the Literature." *Library Acquisitions: Practice & Theory* 8, no.1 (1984): 65–76.

Preservation

Atkinson, Ross. "Preservation and Collection Development: Toward a Political Synthesis." *Journal of Academic Librarianship* 16 (May 1990): 98–103.

_____. "Selection for Preservation: A Materialistic Approach." *Library Resources & Technical Services* 30 (October/December 1986): 341–353.

Byrnes, Margaret. "Preservation and Collection Management: Some Common Concerns." *Collection Building* 9, no.3–4 (1989): 39–45.

Child, Margaret S. "Further Thoughts on 'Selection for Preservation: A Materialistic Approach.'" *Library Resources & Technical Services* 30 (October/December 1986): 354–362.

_____. "Selection for Preservation." In *Advances in Preservation and Access* 1 (1992): 147–158.

Gertz, Janet E., Charlotte B. Brown, and Jane Beebe. "Preservation Analysis and the Brittle Book Problem in College Libraries: The Identification of Research Level Collections and Their Implications." *College & Research Libraries* 54 (May 1993): 227–239.

Hamilton, Marsha J. *Guide to Preservation in Acquisition Processing.* ALCTS Acquisition Guidelines, no. 8. Chicago: American Library Association, 1993.

Hazen, Dan C. "Collection Development, Collection Management, and Preservation." *Library Resources & Technical Services* 26 (January/March 1982): 3–11.

_____. "Preservation in Poverty and Plenty: Policy Issues for the 1990s." *Journal of Academic Librarianship* 15 (January 1990): 344–351.

Motylewski, Karin, and Mary Elizabeth Ruwell. "Preservation and Conservation: Complementary Needs for Libraries and Archives." In *Advances in Preservation and Access* 1 (1992): 213–226.

Ogden, Barclay. "Preservation Selection and Treatment Options." In *Meeting the Preservation Challenge,* 38–42. Ed. Jan Merrill-Oldham. Washington: ARL, 1988.

Tomer, Christinger. "Identification, Evaluation, and Selection of Books for Preservation." *Collection Management* 3, no.1 (1979): 45–54.

Walker, Gay. "Preservation Decision-making and Archival Photocopying." *Restaurator* 8, no.1 (1987): 40–51.

_____. "Preserving the Intellectual Content of Deteriorated Library Materials." In *The Preservation Challenge: A Guide to Conserving Library Materials,* by Carolyn Clark Morrow, 93–113. White Plains, N.Y.: Knowledge Industry Publications, 1983.

Collection Review, Deselection, Storage

Guide to Review of Library Collections: Preservation, Storage, and Withdrawal. Subcommittee on Review of Collections, Collection Management and Development Committee, Resources Section, Association for Library Collections & Technical Services, Lenore Clark, ed. Collection Management and Development Guides, no. 5. Chicago: American Library Association, 1991.

Kovacs, Beatrice. "The Impact of Weeding on Collection Development: Sci-Tech Collections vs. General Collections." *Science & Technology Libraries* 9, no.3 (1989): 25–36.

Metz, Paul. "Thirteen Steps to Avoiding Bad Luck in a Serials Cancellation Project." *Journal of Academic Librarianship* 18 (May 1992): 76–82.

Pierce, Syndey J., ed. *Weeding and Maintenance of Reference Collections.* New York: Haworth Press, 1990. Also published in *Reference Librarian,* no. 29 (1990).

Schlachter, Gail. "Obsolescence, Weeding, and Bibliographic Love Canals." *RQ* 28 (Fall 1988): 7–8.

Other Sources

SPEC Kits. Produced by the Association of Research Libraries' Office of Management Studies, Systems and Procedures Exchange Center, these periodic publications draw upon surveys of practice in actual research library settings to offer practical advice on policies and procedures relating to topics relevant to collection management and staff development. For a listing of the titles available contact: Association of Research Libraries, 1527 New Hampshire Avenue, NW, Washington, DC 20036 (tel.: 202-232-2466).